THE GHOUTA CHEMICAL ATTACKS OF 2013 AND THE END OF THE ARAB SPRING IN SYRIA

PIOTR PIETRZAK

Sofia 2023

Piotr Pietrzak

The Ghouta Chemical Attacks of 2013 and the End of the Arab Spring in Syria

Sofia: ***Dulce Bellum Inexpertis*** Press

ISBN: 9798422864256

This page is intentionally left blank

Introduction

This publication brings to the fore several sociopolitical and legal dimensions related to the international response to the Ghouta chemical attacks on the 21ˢᵗ of August 2013 – the date that ultimately signifies the beginning of the end of the Arab Spring in Syria and the beginning of the new phase that led the actors involved in the local theater of war to a slippery slope of a civil war in Syria.

From my perspective, this deadly chemical assault accounts for one of the most important events that defined the way the international community has dealt with the Syrian Arab Spring, for, according to several influential accounts, the magnitude of this attack clearly transcended the inviolability of the nation-state. Yet, despite gathering compelling prima facie evidence that this attack was linked to Bashar al-Assad's loyalists, the expected full-blown military retaliation against his regime did not occur. The Syrian regime did not face any severe consequences for its actions except for being exposed to the discomfort of temporary international sanctions that obliged the regime to relinquish its chemical weapons arsenal under international supervision.

We know today that despite the promised full cooperation from Syrian officials, the mandate to relinquish all illegal weapons of mass destruction was fulfilled only to a limited extent, and soon afterward, Syria became the site of a number of regime chemical attacks, at least up until early 2019.[1] Morgan Ortagus from the US State Department claims that "the Assad regime has used chemical weapons on its own people at least 50 times since the conflict began" (Ortagus, 2020).

How did a nationwide uprising evolve into a civil war?

After unsuccessful negotiations between opposition leaders and the Syrian government in 2011, Syrian President Bashar al-Assad decided to use disproportional force against peaceful demonstrators. That response caused a nationwide uprising that steadily evolved into a civil war. This was partly due to the fact that the moderate rebels

---

[1] See the reported chemical weapons attacks in: Al-Hasakah on 28 June 2015, Mare' on 1 September 2015, Sheikh Maqsood on 7 April 2016, Eastern Ghouta on 15 June 2016, Aleppo on 10 August 2016, Dandaniya on 25 August 2016, Kafr Zita on 1 October 2016, Sheikh Maqsood on 8 October 2016, Sheikh Maqsood on 25 November 2016, Wadi Barada on 8 January 2017, Al-Lataminah between 25 and 30 March 2017, Hbit on 3 April 2017, Khan Shaykhun on 4 April 2017, Douma on 11 January 2018, East Ghouta on 22 January 2018, Douma on 1 February 2018, Saraqeb on 4 February 2018, Aranda, Afrin on 16 February 2018, Douma on 26 February 2018, Douma on 7 April 2018, Aleppo on 24 November 2018, and Kabana on 19 May 2019. For more information in this respect, refer to similar reports prepared by the Organization for the Prohibition of Chemical Weapons (OPCW), United Nations Human Rights Council (UNHRC), and Human Rights Watch (HRW).

who were predominantly fighting for **the Free Syrian Army** were not strong enough to defeat Assad on their own and proved reluctant to offer the Kurds any significant political concessions in exchange for their support in the fight at the beginning of the uprising.

> **Free Syrian Army** (FSA) is a resistance force and paramilitary group operating as an umbrella of various Syria's opposition groups that was established to protect civilian populations during protests. Over the time, however, the nature of the opposition's struggle rapidly changed from a nonviolent or retaliatory anti-regime action to a multi-layered military confrontation with the loyalists supporting Bashar al-Assad. Some of these groups came under the working umbrella of the FSA. The main goal of this organization was that united these groups was an aspiration to remove Bashar al-Assad from power and to replace him with a leader who would respect the Syrian constitution, add more accountability and transparency to the Syrian political system, and strengthen the mechanisms designed to preserve rule of law. The other main goals and objectives of the FSA included releasing political prisoners, supporting army defections, and bringing to justice all those responsible for killing Syrians, destroying Syria, and displacing its people. The majority of its members were civilians, grassroots organizers, and defectors from the Syrian army. In this respect it has to be mentioned that most FSA members did not

undergo any military training, and as such were poorly armed, poorly trained, visibly outgunned, and lacked a central plan or strategy that could help them to oust the regime from power. For these reasons, it was challenging to unify the groups and brigades operating under this umbrella in a manner that would turn them into a regular army. The other problem that the FSA's leaders faced was the fact that they struggled to establish a centralized operational chain of command throughout most of the initial stage of the uprising and for this reason their actions were more spontaneous than strategic, more predictable than original. The FSA fight against the regime looked more like a confrontation between David and Goliath than a contest of equal forces. (Pietrzak 2019b, p. 48–52).

By the time the moderate rebels realized that foreign fighters from these organizations outnumbered them, it was too late, as they started presenting much better organizational skills, motivation, determination, and unlimited resources in dealing with their political opponents. That is precisely how the Arab Spring in Syria started dying out and the civil war in the country started. The conflict was transformed into a ferocious proxy war the moment the Syrians themselves no longer had the ability to decide about their own matters, as the future of their country was placed in the hands of those more interested in pursuing their own political objectives instead of helping them find a way to resolve similar confrontations. This is already a reality, as it is unlikely that the future of Syria and the fate of the Syrian people will be decided in Syria since the most influential military powers in the global architecture of power have their interests in the region, and they don't hesitate to pursue their goals and objectives at the expense of the smaller players. By the middle of 2012, the situation in Syria had further deteriorated with third parties joining the conflict such as al Qaeda-linked affiliates from the **al Nusra Front** and the **Islamic State of Iraq and Levant (ISIS*)**, which have tried to use the situation in this country to pursue their own political goals and objectives that were inconsistent with the goals and objectives of those who started the Syrian uprising in the first place.

> * When we approach issues related to **ISIS**'s *modus operandi* we need to acknowledge that the Syrian uprising coincided with the civil war in neighboring Iraq and this very fact did not help make things easier for the fight for freedom of the moderate Syrian opposition. As a matter of fact, the security vacuums created in neighboring Iraq started spreading into Syria and had a very detrimental effect ever since early 2012 and affected deeply the way the moderate rebels and the Kurdish Peshmerga operated in this region. Despite this, the moment the self-proclaimed caliph of the Islamic State, **Abu Bakr al-Baghdadi,**[2] made

[2] After the death of **Abu Bakr al-Baghdadi, Abu Ibrahim al-Hashimi al-Qurashi** replaced him as a leader of the Islamic State.

the decision to extend the area of his operations to the liberated territories in Syria, the jihadist cells started mushrooming out of thin air in the eastern and northern parts of the country and started turning into a major factor (Hassan 2020; Khatib 2019). y the end of 2013, in just its first few months of operations in Syria, ISIS managed to establish not only a military presence in northern parts of Syria, but also a

For more information in this respect please see: "Al Mawla: new ISIS leader has a reputation for brutality. Little is known about the man who replaced Abu Bakr Al Baghdadi, who was killed in a US raid in February 2022.

On 3 February 2022, U.S. President Joe Biden announced took a counterterrorism operation in Atme, resulting in the death of **Abu Ibrahim al-Hashimi al-Qurashi.**

Deutsche Welle stated that Abu Ibrahim al-Hashimi al-Qurayshi would be difficult to replace, as many potential leaders had died in the years preceding Al-Qurashi's death.

On 9 February, Egyptian newspaper **Al-Watan** suggested the following individuals as likely candidates for the position:

- **Mu'tazz Nu'man Abdul-Nayef al-Jabbouri**
- **Ziad Jawhar Abdullah**
- **Bashar Khattab Ghazal al-Samidi**
- **Abu Hamzah al-Qurashi al-Muhajir**
- **Nayif Hamad Shayya'**

Please see: Farghali, Maher. "Who Will Succeed Hajj Qardash?" *Al Arabiya English,* February 8, 2022. https://english.alarabiya.net/in-translation/2022/02/09/Who-will-succeed-Hajj-Qardash-.

For more information please see: Pietrzak, Piotr [Forthcoming 2023] *States' use of force against International Terrorist Organizations.*

mini-empire stretching hundreds of kilometers from the outskirts of the Syrian city of Aleppo to the Iraqi cities of Mosul, Kirkuk, and Fallujah. But these impressive territorial acquisitions came at a hefty human price to the civilian population at large of Syria and Iraq as a sizable proportion of them personally experienced the seriousness of al-Baghdadi's declarations. Indeed, the jihadist groups operating under his command have been brutal and ruthless and have shown no regard for the well-being of their civilian populations. Furthermore, they purposefully used civilians as hostages and human shields. There were also examples of beheading, stoning, burning alive, and crucifying those who showed any opposition to ISIS's conquest (Chappell 2014; Dearden, 2017; Human Rights Watch 2017; Gardner 2015).

Meanwhile, **Al-Nusra Front** (known also as Jabhat al-Nusra, or Jabhat Fatah al-Sham) entered Syria in the early months of 2012 and declared that its primary objective was to play a role in removing the Assad government from power. Its leader, the self-proclaimed emir who goes by the name **of Abū Muhammad al-Jūlānī,** made a promise to contribute to the overall fighting efforts of all groups present in Syria to fulfill this goal. It was later reported that there is a far higher proportion of foreign fighters within al Nusra Front ranks than indigenous fighters in comparison with the Free Syrian Army, but this proportion was much lower than amongst the ISIS fighters".

Direct quote from my recent article (Pietrzak, 2019b, p. 55–58).

By early 2013 the situation in Syria started bearing resemblance to the hostile environment of Italian city-states and principalities before the 19th century Risorgimento. Under these conditions, Syria became a place of war of everyone against everyone (*Bellum omnium contra omnes*). President Assad turned to Nicolo Machiavelli for advice, and the jihadists from al Nusra Front and the Islamic State of Iraq and Levant (ISIS) are comparable to Pope Alexander VI and Giuseppe Borgia, as they shared a vision of expanding the areas under their sway into extensive and powerful ecclesiastical states that would have dominated the region, while the moderate commanders from rebel groups and battalions fighting under the umbrella of the **Free Syrian Army** were reduced to the status of disunited feuding Italian heads of families that could hold substantial political power if they learned how to work together, but their lack of ability to cooperate consigned them to the position of political pawns positioned in disadvantageous squares between the pieces that matter on the larger chessboard of regional politics.

The Ghouta Chemical attack happened exactly at the beginning of this chaotic period in Syrian history on 21 August 2013. On that day, Syria and the entire international community witnessed one of the deadliest chemical weapons attacks in recent history[3] and one of the most blatant examples of intentional human rights abuses orchestrated during the Syrian conflict (2011-present). This date signifies the beginning of the end of the Arab Spring in Syria and the beginning of the new phase that led the actors involved in the local theater of war to a slippery slope of a civil war in Syria.

In general, it is easier to prevent than to punish actual human rights abuses, but this observation (however accurate it may be) does not resolve our main issue here. **Contemporary history is full of examples proving that it is extremely difficult to establish a deterrent or sanction strong enough to discourage all potential violators from committing human rights abuses around the world.** For all individuals to be equally accountable for their actions, they need to feel the threat of the most extreme punishment possible. Still, it is only rhetoric, as even if the death penalty were allowed under exceptional circumstances, all of these mass murderers should expect the same very treatment as that which they imposed on millions of their fellow citizens. However, if the international community were in fact about to inflict on these mass murderers the very same inhuman death penalty, we would need to ask ourselves what would constitute an

---

[3] Since the end of World War II, chemical weapons have reportedly been used in only a few cases, notably by Iraq in the 1980s against Iran. For more information, please see: (CWC Review Conference for 2013, 2008 and 2003).

appropriate punishment for those people, given that one is simply not able to multiply the number of victims of these leaders and impose on them a higher or a lower degree of capital punishment. In general, whatever we do, **one can face just one death penalty,** so the actual imbalance between the crimes committed and the penalties faced would always remain very high. All those dilemmas and the way we respond to them have a direct impact on our deliberations on the scope of human rights protection in contemporary conflict zones, its enforceability, and the roles and sources of international law. If the main role of international law is to promote global peace, prosperity, and the human rights of each human being in the world, it should be accompanied by very strong institutions capable of guarding global peace and security and punishing those active and already passive war criminals that are at large for the crimes they have committed. As we know, however, international practice **has clearly illustrated that the international legislator has not been properly equipped with the necessary tools to force or persuade every government to follow the rule of law in this case,** and the Syrian conflict is a perfect example of the nature of this limitation.

The subject of the precise chronological account of the situation in Syria and Iraqi in 2013[4] is too

---

[4] For more information regarding A Bellingcat Report & A Report by Armament Research Services please see (Chemical Weapons Attack in Eastern Ghouta 2020 & HUMAN RIGHTS WATCH.

important and too complicated to be discussed in a parenthesis, for, in a way, the pluralization and radicalization experienced in this borderland is consistent with the patterns of the deterioration unleashed by al-Qaeda and the Taliban[5] in the Afghan-Pakistani borderland and Boko Haram's[6] actions in the borderland of Nigeria, Chad, and Cameroon. In essence, the jihadists from all these theaters of war must have been using the same cross-border playbook, some sort of hide-and-seek strategy in their fight against the local authorities in Syria, Iraq, Pakistan, and Afghanistan, as well as Nigeria, Chad, and Cameroon.

This is, however, not the subject of this inquiry, and I promise to discuss this burning issue elsewhere. For now, I intend to focus predominantly on the international community's response to the Ghouta chemical attack of 2013, for this attack and the international response to it or lack thereof can be seen as one of the most negative outcomes of this conflict from the perspective of the international community. This inaction has contributed significantly to the growing disillusionment as to the role of the

(Organization). 2013).

[5] For more information about al-Qaeda in Afghanistan and Pakistan please see: (Kugelman, 2022; Gul 2022; Mir *at al*, 2022; Baloch, 2022; Sayed, 2020; Chishti 2014; Roggio 2006).

[6] For more information about Boko Haram in Chad, Nigeria please see: (Vasina *at al,* 2021; Kindzeka 2021. Human Rights Watch: Report from Nairobi 2021; Tayo 2022; Eizenga 2021; ACAPS 2022; Comolli 2017; Curie *at al.* 2020; Anyadike 2022; Unicef. 2022).

international community and the United Nations in both Syria and the broader region.

It was the right thing to do to form the US-led coalition that intervened against ISIS's orchestrated genocidal campaign against the region's more vulnerable minorities in 2014 in Iraq.

Back then, all members of the UNSC decided to authorize the use of military force against the members of the Islamic State, it was a positive outcome, for it clearly indicated that the international community was ready to live up to expectations and carry out their responsibilities for global peace and security as the humanitarian situation in both countries deteriorated because of the activity of this terrorist group. In this respect, however, we need to remember that the US-led intervention against ISIS has mainly focused on the territory of Iraq and dealing with these organizations in Syria was largely disregarded at least until 2015. That is when Russia's intervention in the country began, which was less motivated by the necessity of fighting against radical jihadist groups and more by support for the regime of Bashar al-Assad and his inner circle.

But staying mostly idle on the outskirts of the Syrian conflict between 2013 and 2014 was particularly counterproductive from the humanitarian perspective, for it contributed to extended human suffering in both Syria and Iraq in the following years. This relates to an inadvertent consequence of the lack of an adequate response to the perpetrators of the forbidden chemical weapons attacks in 2013, for they ultimately killed the spirit of the Arab Spring in that country, softened the moderate rebels' resolve in Syria, and strengthened Assad's position in relation to his political opponents. Furthermore, the lack of international response also produced more disillusionment among both the opposition fighters and potential recruits, for it gave them the impression that joining the Islamic State in Syria and Iraq or the al-Nusra Front (groups still not accused of genocidal actions in mid-2013 and whose full radicalization happened at the end of the year) would yield more results, for it was apparent that the Free Syrian Army no longer enjoyed Western support. One can argue that an unintended consequence of this far-reaching restraint of Western powers in Syria also resulted in the further deterioration into full-blown civil war in both countries in the following years and may have inspired Putin to intervene in September 2015 on behalf of Syria's dictator - in this instance, a fully-earned pejorative (Washington Post's Editorial Board (2020).

In this respect I also argue that had the international community pursued different goals and objectives in response to the Ghouta attacks, some of the above-mentioned negative outcomes might have been avoided, and the local conflict zone in Syria would not have deteriorated into multiple military confrontations between various small and more sizable groups. However, there was no political will to intervene against the Syrian regime in 2013 due to the fear that the local balance of power was already very shaky. In recent weeks the moderate fighters had given their all in their fight against Assad and they had made several noticeable advances, but their resolve had been significantly weakened by more than two years of intense fighting during the early stages of the uprising. That is why it was expected that Assad's removal from power at that stage of the uprising would not yield the expected outcome in the long run. There was simply no guarantee that the moderates would be capable of stopping any future jihadist takeover of Syria in the following months or years.

Meanwhile, it is important to point out that as of today, the Syrian conflict is slowly but surely heading to its inevitable conclusion, but no matter what the future holds for this country, Syria has suffered an unimaginable scale of destruction and displacement (Shaoul, 2014), that was caused by multiple actors during the last eleven years. In the end, there are no winners, only losers, of this conflict. Assad, having defeated his political enemies, did not win the war but survived it. Yet he is emerging from this confrontation as possibly the biggest loser, for his political credibility is virtually non-existent due to his regime's war crimes and various human rights abuses, and this is particularly true due to his regime's involvement in the Ghouta Attack of 2013.

As much as the Syrian regime surely took these abuses to an extreme, it must be admitted that a huge proportion of successive governments in the broader Middle East and North Africa partly share the blame for the status quo in this respect. The way the recent developments in Libya, Yemen, Egypt, Saudi Arabia, Bahrain, Iran, Israel, and, of course, Syria and Iraq have unfolded and the way local regimes have reacted to them indicate that it is very unlikely that the overall conditions for human rights improvement will improve any time soon. Understandably, in the eyes of a significant proportion of locals as well as a number of Western scholars, out of the recent events in this part of the world, the closest to a manifestation of the desire for and a trigger for a positive change and a new beginning for the entire region were the Arab Spring events (Hassan 2020; Pietrzak 2021a).

In this instance, I am convinced that Assad loyalists masterminded and undertook this lethal attack and suggest that their involvement can be proven with a probable cause argument (derived from Roman orator Cicero's expression *cui bono?*, meaning "to whose benefit?"), for it explains a great deal about the predicament that the Syrian regime was facing during this stage of the confrontation with moderate rebels and clearly implicates Assad loyalists in the attack. We don't know who gave the order or "pulled the trigger", but it must have been someone from his inner circle acting in accordance with a broader military and political rationale of keeping Assad's regime in power in Syria.

Naturally, one cannot prove this hypothesis beyond a reasonable doubt, for there is no tangible evidence proving the assertion, but as of early 2013, the situation in Syria was quickly slipping out of Assad's control, and he must have been preoccupied with his own political survival to the extent that he could not be discouraged from orchestrating this deadly assault because of some humanitarian consideration such as caring about the high number of civilians in these areas (Naturally, now, in 2023, regime change seems to be a very remote possibility and wishful thinking, but back in the beginning of 2013, it was reported that Assad was heading for a fall in Syria as the shrinking of the territory of his "Regime-stan" was a daily occurrence. But as it quickly turned out, he also employed a strategy of consolidating his grip on power in the core of Syria around Damascus, Hama, Homs, Latakia and parts of Aleppo in 2013, which paid off after 2015, when his regime got unexpected assistance from the Russians).

Just days before the attacks, it was reported that Assad was running out of options, his conventional arsenal was heavily depleted, and the members of the moderate opposition were quickly approaching Damascus,[7] and, as it happened, the strategically important Ghouta suburban

---

[7] In this instance we can draw a certain analogy with the speed of the advancement of ISIS towards Mosul and the Free Syrian Army march towards Damascus in 2012 and 2013. The future of the Middle East lay in the hands of the anti-ISIS Coalition combating the jihadist forces in Mosul.

neighborhood of Damascus just happened to be in their way before they could advance another 15-17 km to the governmental compounds in the country's capital. The international media as well as the Syrian regime had justified reasons to believe that from a conventional perspective, this campaign was destined to be successful, meaning that the opposition forces were perfectly capable of ousting Assad and replacing his doomed regime with the government-in-waiting. That is exactly when the chemical attack of 2013 occurred, so on this basis, it can be plausibly argued that this attack against the opposition forces who resided in these heavily populated civilian areas of Ghouta must have been politically and strategically motivated.

Moreover, the use of forbidden chemical agents in Ghouta (that can be defined as a weapon of mass destruction) benefited the regime in the following years, for sarin gas proved to be the only "successful" means of dealing with the opposition and putting an end to the successful campaign of the Free Syrian Army (FSA) "marching" towards the capital city of Damascus. This was also the only "effective" strategy to reinforce Assad's position in relation to the opposition and was consistent with earlier chemical attacks unleashed against the FSA on a much smaller scale. Unfortunately, this was just another lowering of the standards in non-existent rules of engagement, for Assad had been unleashing a strategy of annihilation against his political enemies since 2011.

The Syrian regime has never officially claimed any direct or indirect responsibility for the Ghouta attack,[8] but the intent here is clear, for it relates to the basic military principle of using all means necessary to halt the enemy's advances towards the capital and closing all potential gateways that might lead to inevitable success. If we apply this military rationale to these deliberations, he who takes the capital is the ultimate winner of any war.

Losing Damascus was something that Assad could not afford, for his political legitimacy was based on keeping a strong grip on power in Syria and in the capital. Surely, his Machiavellian advisors must have persuaded him to do everything in their power to protect his rule, even if it meant using chemical weapons against fellow citizens. The fact that the strategically important region of Ghouta ended up in the hands of the FSA in the first place must have been such an unexpected outcome that it must have caused the regime a lot of distress. That the Syrian army was not able to win it back in a conventional manner may also suggest that the perpetrators of the chemical attacks (if they were indeed related to the Assad regime) must have been strongly interested in changing this situation at any cost. As much as

[8] According to **Human Rights Watch Report** (2013), the evidence suggests that the rockets originated from the area around Mezzeh Military Airport, which is near Air Force Intelligence, a Republican Guard base, and the 4th Division base (Civil Rights Defenders *et al*, 2013; Higgins, 2014).

Syrian or Russian propaganda argued the contrary, it was difficult to frame the narrative in a way to suggest that the FSA would want to attack their own positions in Ghouta, especially since they had fought such a long time to reach that point. So, considering all those deliberations, we can make an educated guess and a working hypothesis that Assad's loyalists were behind these attacks, for they were desperate enough to pursue this strategy at any cost, even at the expense of a significant number of civilian lives.

The international community's response to the Ghouta attacks

The way in which the international community responded to the Ghouta crisis and to the Syrian conflict, in general, can be partly explained by the way the international legal system works, for it is still heavily influenced by Max Weber's doctrine that **the state owns a monopoly on violence**, which is supported by the principle of non-intervention in the internal affairs of independent international actors. This legal institutional basis is underpinned by the United Nations Security Council's position as the ultimate arbiter that is legally allowed to decide when the non-intervention doctrine should be bypassed and under what circumstances. Naturally, we also need to indicate the existence of **the Responsibility to Protect (R2P) Doctrine**[9] (one of the most recent additions to the way humanitarian response law functions), for it reinterprets the traditional non-interventionist standpoint of the international community to a large extent. The use of R2P is still rather selective because such influential states as Russia and China show a far-reaching skepticism to the R2P's arbitrary use in the international realm. This is due to its use during the Libyan crisis of 2011.[10] That being said, the development of the situation in Syria in 2013 shocked international legislators, for a regime that had used illegal weapons of mass destruction could not be brought to justice. Its biggest international supporter, Putin, showed a complete and unconditional loyalty[11] by stopping every single act of the international community that would have brought his Syrian counterpart to justice despite the majority of members of the international community having withdrawn their recognition of

---

[9] **The Responsibility to Protect Doctrine** is the latest and modest but surely advantageous legal innovation that was introduced by international legislators to prioritize human rights protection over the laws protecting the territorial integrity and sovereignty of any given state, especially in instances in which a rogue regime attempts to hide under the shield of sovereignty (Genser & Cotler 2012; Thakur & Maley 2015, p. 3–78).

[10] I have explained this controversy in detail in a recent paper (Pietrzak 2019a).

[11] Ümit Seven suggests in this respect that the Russian Federation has provided the Syrian President Bashar al Assad with a diplomatic shield and a very adaptive supportive strategy in their broader game with the West (Seven, 2022), this finding is consistent with my observations regarding this issue published in (Pietrzak 2013; Pietrzak 2018, p. 101 - 116; Pietrzak 2019a; Pietrzak 2019b, p. 34–98; Pietrzak 2021a, p. 155-178; Pietrzak 2021b, p. 53-84).

Assad's regime and no longer considering him to be the legitimate ruler of Syria.[12]

[12] Bashar al-Assad's legitimacy may be questioned, but he still governs Syria, and his regime extends its power over the majority of the country. Fabrice Balanche maintains that "by ceding control of its borders and airspace to various foreign actors, the regime has essentially resigned itself to a limited but potentially durable existence for the long term." (Balanche 2021).

Why we should assign such significance to this singular chemical attack when there had already been so much blood spilled in Syria?

Surely, the Ghouta attack was not the first time that the Assad regime decided to treat its fellow citizens as cannon fodder, for there are countless examples suggesting that the Syrian president committed various crimes against humanity before 2011, persecuting his political opponents and forcing his fellow citizens to endure all sorts of suffering, ill-treatment, discrimination, and denials of freedom. So, on this basis, one could ask why this situation was any different from previous assaults inflicted on the civilian population of Syria by the Assad regime. On this occasion, the situation was different, as the magnitude of this attack clearly transcended the inviolability of the nation-state, for it was probably one of the deadliest chemical attacks since the Iran-Iraq War (1980-1988). It resulted in the loss of a significant number of lives (depending on the calculations, between 281 and 1729 casualties (Baker *et al*, 2013; Chulov *et all* 2013; Borger, 2013)), and those people were killed with illegal weapons of mass destruction forbidden by the international community. Even though there was no clear admission of guilt, many Western political commentators quickly "connected the dots" and made an educated guess suggesting that it was Assad's loyalists who were directly responsible for the use of deadly sarin gas in the attacks. Yet, despite the clear declarations that such or any similar attack would be seen as crossing a red line, the international community did not respond adequately to this blatant example of human rights violations, as gassing civilians is strongly forbidden by international law.

The international community stood at the brink of pursuing a military action against the Syrian regime at least several times after the outbreak of the Syrian Arab Spring in 2011. Another example occurred when the United Nations Security Council (UNSC) deliberated on the draft resolution S/2012/77 on Syria in February 2012, but Russia and China decided to veto it. For more information in this respect please see: (Pietrzak 2013; Pietrzak 2019a; Pietrzak 2019b, p. 34–98; Pietrzak 2021a, p. 155-178).

How Assad got away with the Ghouta Chemical Attacks

As much as the influential members of the international community have shown a far-reaching reluctance to actively engage in the resolution of the Syrian conflict in the past, between 2011 and 2013, the situation was different, as the events in Ghouta were not just about another conflict in the Middle East – they were about the use of chemical weapons and about making sure that we as an international community would preserve our capability of deterring their use elsewhere.

This logic can be found in the Kantian deontology that suggests that human beings are not mere objects—they are persons who are worthy of respect and who must be treated as such, the Augustinian *jus belli justi* principle suggests that in military conflict parties are allowed to use proportional power to attain their political goals and objectives. So, as a matter of principle, it was in the international community's interest to respond to these attacks with a full retaliation for an unchecked use of deadly chemical weapons in one place in the world which would produce similar misuses of illegal chemical weapons elsewhere.

According to the Geneva Protocol of 1925, the use, possession, and manufacture of chemical weapons is prohibited, and every member of the international community should comply with the relevant treaties preventing their use. Naturally, this piece of legislation is selectively interpreted, for even permanent members of the UNSC have had in their possession large stockpiles of chemical weapons, but the main emphasis in this debate is directed towards the concept of their use in military conflict rather than their possession.

In this respect, we need to remember that the use of chemical weapons is also prohibited by the Universal Declaration of Human Rights of 1945, the UN Charter of 1945, and the UN Responsibility to Protect (R2P) Doctrine of 2005 due to the fact that **these laws tend to render the principles of state sovereignty and non-interference in the internal affairs of other international actors inferior to universal human rights.** The R2P is also very clear in stating that state sovereignty should be understood in a much broader sense than we are used to and that any contemporary leader who puts the rights of his fellow citizens in danger or is a threat to their existence should be held accountable for his actions and should not be allowed to hide behind the shield of state sovereignty to escape justice.

Furthermore, the magnitude of the Ghouta Chemical Attack was such that it made headlines and caused significant global outrage among world leaders including US President Barack Obama, British Prime Minister David Cameron, and French President Francois Hollande, who declared that they would seriously consider retaliatory military action against the Syrian regime. Given the depravity Assad had displayed and the moral outrage at using chemical weapons to kill innocents, there was a strong case for permitting the expected military intervention, especially considering that in the direct aftermath of the events of 21 August 2013, the vast majority of

Western decision-makers were more keen to intervene in Syria than at any prior point.

In this respect it is worth emphasizing that whilst the full scope of the clandestine effort to train opposition fighters in Syria remains unclear, we know for certain that from the very beginning in early 2012 the US supplied the moderate rebels of the Free Syrian Army with non-lethal aid, but by the middle of 2013 the US government, at the direction of US President Barack Obama, began the so-called Operation Timber Sycamore aimed at providing US help to the anti-government forces of the Free Syrian Army and selected independent brigades in Syria with training, cash, logistical support, and intelligence. At its peak, the Central Intelligence Agency that oversaw these operations was authorized to spend up to $1 billion annually on the effort to arm and train moderate Syrian rebels, predominantly under a growing secret program run by the CIA in Jordan and Turkey. This support was stopped by Russia, whose military offensive focused predominantly on the CIA-backed fighters battling Syrian government troops, pounding the areas under their control with intense air strikes until the arrival of the new administration in the White House. According to the New York Times, upon CIA director Mike Pompeo's recommendations, Donald Trump put an end to the costliest covert action programs in the history of the CIA in the beginning of 2017. Schmitt, Rosenberg, Apuzzo, (2017).

Still, in the direct aftermath of the Ghouta attacks, the US government froze every channel of communication between Washington and Damascus and clearly suggested the perpetrator of the attack was the Syrian regime. Still, despite his previous declarations, President Barack Obama made it clear that the US would not respond in a unilateral fashion against the regime to deter any chemical weapons aggression in the future, and he called on the international community to authorize a retaliatory action against Assad. From a legal perspective, the only international body that could authorize such a collective intervention was the United Nations Security Council, but one of its permanent members, Russia, was also a great ally of Assad and had vetoed similar previous initiatives.

The international community shows no appetite to intervene in Syrian on a humanitarian basis. It was suggested that the Syrian president should be brought to justice for making a mockery of the rule of international law, but Assad happened to have a powerful Russian friend, for, in the end, the UNSC decided to display far-reaching restraint in its response to the events in Syria, which ultimately allowed him to hide behind the shield of his country's sovereignty.

The situation in Syria has been further complicated by the fact that it is not just a local confrontation, since some of the most influential military powers in the global architecture of power, Russia and the US, have shown a strong propensity to pursue their respective objectives there. Traditionally they both have a compelling interest in the region, so when one party shows no interest in stepping in, the other party generally takes advantage of the situation. That is precisely what happened in Syria in 2015. As we have seen, Russia was very much invested in Syria, as it had been propping up Assad's regime since the outbreak of the Arab Spring in 2011. If it had not been for Moscow's assistance, it would have been difficult for Bashar al-Assad to preserve his power in Syria beyond 2015. Thanks to his powerful friends, Assad was able to enjoy a strong sense of security and most probably will stay in power, but the question remains as to what will happen after the Syrian conflict finishes. Will Russia remain actively interested in rebuilding this country from the ashes of conflict or will its interest in backing the regime diminish significantly?

So even though it was clearly suggested before August 2013 that had the "butcher of Damascus" used chemical weapons, he would follow in Saddam Hussein's and Muammar Gadhafi's footsteps, he did not, for he happened to have much more reliable allies. It was clearly not a unique occurrence; it was part of a pattern of Russia's behavior to prevent any retaliation against Assad, as shown on a number of occasions during earlier stages of this confrontation.

It is also a well-known fact that were it not in Russia's interest, Assad would not be in power anymore. That is why ever since Russia's intervention in Syria in 2015, Putin did not "discriminate" between targeting foreign-funded jihadist mercenaries in the Iraqi-Syrian borderland (from ISIS, al-Nusra Front) and moderate groups fighting under the shield of the Free Syrian Army operating predominantly in Syria. For sure, in this respect, Moscow did not discriminate between targeting the extremist or the moderate rebels, especially if they wanted to unseat Assad from power. For more information in this respect, please refer to: (Davison & Landis 2018; Deher 2018; Pietrzak 2018, p. 101 – 116; Walt 2015).

In the end, on this occasion, the permanent five members of the UNSC also decided to take more conciliatory measures against the Assad administration that involved forcing him to give up his chemical weapons arsenal and placing his regime under international supervision until this task was completed. This outcome was achieved predominantly thanks to the diplomatic intervention of Russian Foreign Minister Sergei Lavrov, who outmaneuvered his American counterpart in a last attempt to defend Assad in a meeting with his American counterpart John Kerry, suggesting that the Syrian president would be ready to surrender his chemical weapons stockpiles in exchange for averting US retaliation. This was an unprecedented turn of events, as instead of punishing Assad for the actions of the loyalist forces under his command in the Ghouta region, the US and Russia decided to act on behalf of the international community to make a deal with his regime to offer him what later turned out to be impunity in exchange for relinquishing control of Syrian chemical weapons. This, in essence, however, meant something else from a criminal law perspective, for it introduced into international law the notion of plea bargaining, which usually involves the defendant's pleading guilty to a lesser charge, and in exchange, the prosecution (in this case the international community) would recommend some leniency in sentencing. However, in essence, this was a very lenient sentence that involved giving up the right to possession of illegal weapons of mass destruction that should not have been in Assad's arsenal in the first place.

One should not be surprised if the opponents of this "plea deal" were not excited about it because despite having his fingers all over the chemical weapons attack, the Assad regime was suddenly, out of the blue, offered a generous "Get Out of Jail Free" card, and the international community let him get away with the crime in exchange for his chemical weapons arsenal and an inadvertent admission of guilt. If we applied the same standard to criminal law, it would be like offering Lee Harvey Oswald the same deal in exchange for handing in his weapon just after he was caught assassinating President Kennedy in 1963. Such an act of mercy would have put all Kennedy's successors at grave risk. But this is just a highly hypothetical example that has very little to do with the letter of international law or the reality on the ground in Syria in 2013. So, what happened at the negotiating table between the US and Russian teams who acted on behalf of the international community? It seems that the victims of this attack and their families were mugged by this rather peculiar arrangement.

There is a difference between the local criminal code and the letter of international law, as the latter empowers the country's officials to enjoy a certain immunity: presidents, prime ministers, and other influential politicians enjoy certain freedoms and a level of protection that is denied to ordinary citizens. This means that comparing Assad (who potentially authorized the killing of 1300 innocent civilians) and Oswald (who allegedly was responsible for assassinating one of the best public speakers in the history of mankind who happened to be a president) would not be fully adequate. Indeed, it would be more appropriate to employ here a slightly different comparative study, for Assad could be more appropriately compared to Yugoslav President Slobodan Milosevich, General Ratko Mladic, Bosnian Croat military commander Slobodan Praljak, and possibly many other Balkan "leaders" who at the end of their lives faced the same line of questioning at The Hague. Surely, they were never brought to justice in the way the international community would have expected, but at least we have tried to do so.

General Ratko Mladic is infamous for two main cases of modern genocide in Sarajevo while besieged by the Army of Republika Srpska from 5 April 1992 to 29 February 1996 (1425 days) during the Bosnian War. Only in Srebrenica of 1995 (the UN declared that Srebrenica was to be considered to be a safe enclave, but the Dutch UN troops that were meant to defend it abandoned it because of higher commands. Srebrenica was overrun and more than 20,000 Bosniak Muslims were killed. Ratko Mladic guaranteed the safe passage of women and children, but his men hunted down almost every single man of Srebrenica. They were gathered in public places and killed).

In Sarajevo, Ratko Mladic used superior military against civilian populations, not only adults but also children, as a matter of fact, according to Fikret Grabovica, president of the Association of Murdered Families and Children, during the Bosnia war, children were deliberately being killed throughout the siege; countless examples prove that each time they were leaving their shelters, whilst playing in groups, children were indiscriminately targeted by Serbian snipers who were encouraged to kill as many children as possible to prevent the Muslim community from restoring its population after the war. It is important to point out that the Serbs are quite rightly blamed for masterminding the outbreak and aggravating and reigniting these hostilities prior to and after the Dayton Agreement of 1995 (which ended the Bosnian War). The Serbian government was also responsible for soaking the entire region in blood and unleashing unthinkable carnage, harassment, starvation, beatings, torture, sexual abuse, mass killing, detentions, forced labor camps, detention centers, war crimes, prosecution, murder, most of the ethnic cleansing, dehumanizing people, and the destruction of mosques. Most of these hostilities were predominantly directed towards the Bosniak Muslim minority mostly inhabiting the territory of Bosnia and Kosovo in the Former Yugoslavia in the 1990s. The deadly actions of the government of Slobodan Milosevich and General **Radko Mladic** (former general found guilty of committing war crimes, crimes against humanity, and genocide) resulted in meadows full of dead people and mass graves all across Bosnia and then Kosovo; the entire region of the Western Balkans is soaked in the blood and suffering of local people, both Muslims, and Christians and this had an effect on the lives of millions of people. For more information, please see: (the United States, and Bill Clinton. 1998; Pietrzak 2021a, p. 77-100).

Meanwhile, the message that Assad received in the aftermath of the 2013 Ghouta attacks was that he could still "enjoy" the "luxury of pounding his foes city by city", leaving them little space to retreat or regroup; he would not be held accountable for the unjust imprisonment or torture of his political opponents[13] if he only promised not to use chemical weapons again, at least not so often. Naturally, we need to admit that although Moscow and Washington were driven by different intentions during the post-Ghouta attack negotiations with the Syrian regime, the Russians wanted to protect the friendly despot from the Middle East at all costs, whilst the US Government was clearly interested in securing destruction of the rest of the chemical weapons in Assad's arsenal or at least placing them under international supervision so no future Syrian would be exposed to chemical attack.

The opponents of the post-Ghouta attack negotiation with Assad emphasized that this deal did not go far enough since it created conditions of impunity for any perpetrator of similar future attacks. It was also emphasized that by agreeing to such a solution, global decision-makers agreed to a silent conspiracy to pretend that nothing significant

[13] In 2015 a Syrian military police photographer who worked for the Assad government for 13 years (whose pseudonym was Caesar) approached the US authorities and offered a disk containing 55,000 smuggled photographs of people who were inhumanly tortured and murdered by the Syrian authorities. His testimony to Congress in 2019 eventually led to mandating an escalation of US pressure in Syria. For more information, please see: (Washington Post's Editorial Board (2020); Human Rights Watch. 2015).

happened at Ghouta if the Assad regime plays by the rules and shows a readiness to relinquish its chemical weapons. Subsequently, it was also maintained that letting Assad get away with this crime seemed like a fundamentally wrong decision from an ethical standpoint as it allowed the responsible party to go unpunished for the crimes committed on the Syrian people.

Why the Western powers decided not to intervene in Syria after the Ghouta Attacks

The parties that were considering retaliation against the Syrian authorities back in 2013 in response to the use of chemical weapons, had they acted in good faith, would most probably have utilized NATO's experience in former Yugoslavia, but this would have meant that such an operation would have had a very militaristic character that would not have prioritized saving Syrian lives, but rather would have entailed a limited bombing campaign against military targets, governmental buildings, or Assad's private residence and bunker. However, from the perspective of the Obama administration, dropping a limited number of bombs on Syrian positions was not a viable option. Neither the US government nor the international community had the intention to deploy 100,000 pairs of boots on the ground to remove Assad from power or to bring the real perpetrators of the attack to justice, for it would have meant opening Pandora's box, as George W. Bush did in Iraq in 2003.

Such an action could not have produced any meaningful outcome that would have satisfied the expectations of those who advocated securing more tangible support for the moderates. Also, any irresponsible use of the US's retaliatory arsenal might have created more harm than good. For these reasons, there was no point in pretending that Washington had obtained some miraculous cure that would have solved all the problems of the Syrian people and removed their leader from power. Instead, what Obama and his Russian counterpart achieved was to put some of the most dangerous weapons of mass destruction in the world under international supervision and to secure the destruction of chemical agents that were destined to be misused, as by mid-2013, the Syrian conflict zone had seen a vast influx of jihadist fighters who had already openly started taking advantage of local chaos to lay the foundations for a mini-state. Within just a few months of the start of its operations in Syria, ISIS had extended its strong military presence from western Iraq to northern Syria, and its leader Abu Bakr al-Baghdadi declared the founding of an Islamic caliphate that at its peak stretched hundreds of kilometers from the Mediterranean coastline of Syria's Latakia to the Iraqi cities of Mosul and Fallujah, controlling a territory of approximately

100,000 km². That is why these should be seen as very positive developments.

Ultimately, the Russian intervention in the Syria conflict in 2015 put an end to this particular type of speculative analysis but cleared the way for employing even more damaging narratives suggesting that Assad had won the conflict. If anything, he barely survived the uprising against his regime, not due to his military genius or any special strategic skills, but thanks to Putin's patronage and desire to keep his Syrian counterpart in power. Another similar interpretation suggests that Russia's intent to keep Assad in power can explain a great deal of why Assad is still in charge of Syria, but it is necessary to emphasize that the US government and the rest of the so-called anti-Assad coalition were not as interested in removing him from office as Russia was in keeping him in power.

The situation in Syria in 2013 and in 2015

When the case of potential intervention in Syria to punish Assad for his actions at Ghouta was discussed, the global architecture of power looked completely different than in September 2015, when Russia intervened in Syria, for no one could seriously question the US's right to call itself the world's first and only global superpower (Brzezinski, 2017). Surely, anyone who followed all of the Lavrov-Kerry meetings (U.S. Mission in Geneva, 2013), at that point saw Russia as the weaker link, for Lavrov had to trick John Kerry into offering Syria the deal of the century; he did not do so from a position of strength.

> Whilst the US Secretary of State John Kerry visited Europe to gather support for the military action, he met with his British counterpart Foreign Secretary William Hague to discuss the best course the leaders of these countries could take to break the international impasse over the Syrian chemical weapons crisis. Soon after this meeting, they organized a press conference to discuss the results of their discussions, but these were overshadowed by the Foreign Secretary being asked whether there was anything that Assad could do to avoid military action in Syria, and he inadvertently suggested that the US would be happy to reconsider its plans to strike the

Syrian authorities if they would hand over the entire Syrian arsenal of chemical weapons within the following week.

These words sounded like one last chance for Assad: a clear ultimatum to hand over all of his chemical weapons within a very short period of time or face retaliatory action; Russian Foreign Minister Sergey Lavrov almost immediately seized on this and organized a news conference where he stated that since there was an initiative here, he would try to persuade the Syrian authorities to comply with this request. Despite the fact that US officials almost immediately tried to deny the import of the statement by suggesting that Kerry was just making a rhetorical argument rather than a serious offer, his Russian counterpart took this statement very seriously. In a matter of hours, Lavrov contacted Syrian Minister of Foreign Affairs Walid Muallem and advised him that the only way the Western military action against Syrian authorities could be averted was if Syria was prepared to give their chemical weapons up and suggested that his country would have to get serious about giving up all its deadly toxins and placing all of its production sites under international control; otherwise Russia would not be able to prevent the Western strikes. The Russian foreign minister also suggested to his Syrian peer that this time the Western leaders seemed to be very determined to get what they wanted; therefore, it would be advisable for the Syrian authorities to consider joining all the required chemical weapons conventions and doing everything possible to comply, as such an offer might never be repeated. It is a given that we will never know the exact content of their conversation, but it seems that Lavrov was very persuasive when he suggested that the Assad government come clean about his entire chemical arsenal due to the fact that Muallem almost immediately organized a press conference and announced that Syria welcomed the Russian initiative and was willing to adhere to all demands of unconditionally handing over its entire arsenal of chemical weapons for their prompt destruction, but he also suggested that it would take them much longer than a week to disarm, as the country was in the middle of civil war.

In the line of the Russian suggestion, the Syrian authorities notified the secretary-general of the United Nations of their intention to apply the Convention on the Prohibition of the Development, Production, Stockpiling, and Use of Chemical Weapons and on their Destruction (hereinafter "the Convention") on 12 September 2013 and handed in their preliminary set of documents containing detailed information including names, types, and quantities of its chemical weapons agents, types of munitions, and location and form of storage, production, and research and development facilities on 19 September 2013 to the Organization for the Prohibition of Chemical Weapons (OPCW).

We don't need to speculate to determine that at that point in the conflict (the end of summer 2013) the Kremlin was still not ready to go all in in Syria. We know for a fact that Putin was not ready to fully engage in the Middle East, as, at that time, he had been preoccupied with the destabilization of Ukraine and drawing the blueprint for the annexation of Crimea, which happened half a year after the Ghouta events in Syria. So, at that time, it looked like the entire weight of the decision-making process related to the developments in Syria lay predominantly on President Obama's shoulders. The entire world was waiting for him to make up his mind with respect to the chemical attacks. In the end, Obama decided to embrace pragmatism and not to intervene in a direct manner in retaliation for these chemical attacks. He was widely criticized for his conservative approach[14] as the only consequences that the Syrian regime faced for its actions in Ghouta were that Assad had to promise to destroy or return to international supervision his entire chemical weapons arsenal. By making such a promise, Assad ultimately averted an international community retaliatory response against his regime, but, as bad as it

[14] The main side effect of this deal was that in its direct aftermath, the people who started the Syrian Arab Spring lost any initiative. Meanwhile, the rapid influx of the jihadist fighters from al Nusra Front, Al Qaeda, and the so-called Islamic State have paradoxically not affected the regime, but rather their ranks. Since the beginning of 2014, global political commentators became more concerned with the growing radicalization of the Syrian and Iraqi theaters of war.

sounds, at that time it was the right course of action for several reasons.

Naturally, all facts suggested that there was little doubt that the regime was responsible for the chemical attacks in Ghouta, and all rationales suggested that the leader who abused his fellow citizens in such a manner could not be trusted, but the fact was that Assad still had tons of chemical agents at his disposal and would not have hesitated to use them as he had already proven on many occasions should his rule be under threat again. From a legal perspective, as it turned out, the Syrian Arab Republic had never ratified any convention that forbids the use of chemical weapons (until September 2013) , and given that the UNSC (due to potential Russia's veto) would have refused to authorize any retaliatory action against the Syrian leader, the Obama Administration and the international community at large had no choice but to engage in further negotiations with those responsible for the Ghouta attacks and hope for the best, which, as a matter of fact, from the broader humanitarian perspective of the security of the entire Middle East, was to find a meaningful way to halt any further proliferation of these weapons throughout the region. So, negotiating with the regime either their ultimate destruction or voluntary surrender under international supervision must have been the goal all along. Such goals as bringing the civil war to a reasonable conclusion or removing Assad from power became secondary, and rightly so.

We need to remember in this case that from a legal perspective since the majority of the countries in the world have made an executive decision to ban the use of chemical weapons, this decision became legally binding for everyone; for by doing so, they have automatically extended the power of this legislation prohibiting the use of chemical weapons to every single country in the world; even those that have not signed a relevant convention were obliged to respect the rule of majority. We need to remember that legal matters and the practical application of international law in conflicts are two different things. So, the negotiating parties who approach such complex matters like enforcing certain rules and regulations on the disparate parties engaged in an ongoing regional conflict need to consider all possibilities on the table.

Unfortunately, it was not only the matter of Russia's vetoing every single piece of international legislation that could authorize any retaliatory actions against the Syrian regime. The other members of the international community simply did not come together to overcome those vetoes. For instance, Syria's neighbors did not decide to come together and involve themselves in the Syrian conflict in a more conciliatory and diplomatic manner. Turkey basically used the Syrian uprising to its own benefit by taking a chance to weaken the

Assad regime, which happened to be Erdogan's eternal enemy. Iraq was too preoccupied with its own internal problems. Jordan at least until 2014 decided to play Switzerland and not openly engage in the conflict. Israel was quite happy that global attention was shifted away from their abuse of the Palestinians and their hawkish policies in the West Bank, whilst Lebanon-based Hezbollah decided to back Assad in a friendly gesture of repaying an old debt for Assad family support during the 30-year-long civil war that lasted until the beginning of 1990s. The local government in Lebanon was too week to engage. So, except for voicing its vocal disapproval of the way the situation in Syria unfolded, the international community did relatively little to stop hostilities, either by authorizing direct military intervention or by suggesting any other meaningful action that would have coerced the involved parties to sit at the negotiation table until the solution could be found. Naturally, this lack of progress in bringing all parties involved to some sort of accommodation resulted in irremediable damage and destruction to the country's cultural heritage and industrial infrastructure and, of course, an unimaginable amount of human suffering.

Still, neither Russia nor the other permanent members of the United Nations Security Council could be blamed for the fact that they had allowed Assad's crimes to go unpunished for more than two years by the middle of 2013, so they should have expected that at some point he would start running out of conventional weapons. They should have offered a more meaningful temporary political solution to the conflict, but they failed at that task and lost their sense of responsibility. Instead of stepping in and separating the feuding sides, as the UNSC had done in Cyprus in 1974, these parties acted in a very cynical and calculated manner by assuming their roles as puppet masters, staging, masterminding, and fighting with some of the poorest people on the planet, employing various mercenaries, foreign fighters, and armies with camouflaged uniforms obedient to the highest bidders, and trying to impose on the Syrian population at large top-down decisions that would shape the future according to their liking. By doing so they have taken from ordinary Syrians the ability to determine their own future.

Syria's leader could have been ousted in the aftermath of August 2013's Ghouta chemical weapons attacks, but the international community settled for Assad's declaration that his regime would give up some of its chemical weapons. A similar development happened in 2014, for the same international coalition that was formed against ISIS did not feel inclined to support the moderate rebels or the Kurdish minority in their quest to remove Assad from power. Surely, in this instance, the global policymakers also acted in accordance with logic suggesting that the potential jihadist takeover of large swaths of land in Syria and Iraq could constitute a much more serious threat than Assad's regime, but there was never any follow-up action once the immediate issues with ISIS were resolved. The Syrian regime was not removed from power despite countless declarations of parties interested in pursuing that objective. It became clear that Assad was going to stay in power for the foreseeable future because Russia, Iran, and Hezbollah supported him and because the moderate rebels were too weak to take any initiative anymore. Meanwhile, the jihadi, Salafi, and Wahhabi foreign fighters who had seriously overstayed their welcome in the Syrian-Iraqi borderland were regrouping or changing their areas of operations.

From the perspective of hindsight, we know that Assad's promises and explanations were largely disingenuous, for soon afterward, Syria became the site of a number of regime chemical attacks, at least up until late 2018 (in this respect, please see the OPCW 2018 Report). Very similar chemical attacks kept happening in Syria until at least the end of 2017, so there was merit to the suggestion that this decision would save hundreds of lives, but when we take into account the scale and scope of all of the prevented chemical attacks that might have otherwise happened with the use of a hundred tons of deadly chemical agents, it has to be admitted that this decision could be seen as a limited success.

The US response to the Khan Shaykhun chemical attacks of 2017

If we were to compare the magnitude and the scope of the Ghouta chemical attack to any other chemical attack after 2013 in Syria, it would be to those of 2017 that occurred in the town of Khan Shaykhun in the Idlib Province and killed at least 86, for regime hands were all over that attack. A day later, the newly-elected US President Donald Trump criticized the Syrian regime for the attack and authorized a swift retaliatory action against the Syrian regime, but the response (59 Tomahawk cruise missiles fired against the Shayrat Airfield, where the warplanes used in these chemical attacks were located) was somewhat limited considering the magnitude of the chemical attacks. One could say that there was hardly any response, considering that it was presented as a strong action against a political player who was already persistent in overusing the chemical agents he found at his disposal at the expense of his fellow citizens just to save his position. What was even more disturbing was that this limited response achieved nothing of substance for the security of the region but rather just showed that Trump was not interested in doing anything beyond striking an unknown military object of minimal strategic importance. To anyone who compares this act of retaliation with previous US interventions in the region in the last twenty years, it must seem a somewhat conservative improvisation compared to what the US Army was really capable of. Also, this response had nothing to do with the concept of humanitarian intervention because of its retaliatory character: it did not intend to save civilian lives. Naturally, the Assad regime should have been penalized for its refusal to adhere to the rules of international law, but responding with only 59 missiles launched towards one of the least strategically important Syrian Air Bases hardly constituted a sufficient response considering the scale of the chemical attacks themselves. Trump's response to the Khan Sheikhoun chemical attacks showed his inability to deal with these human rights abuses in an adequate manner. Trump did not employ the principle of restraint that was characteristic of his predecessor's choice after the Ghouta attacks.

In this respect, it is worth reiterating that both Obama and Trump were perfectly aware that the real improvement of the situation of non-combat populations trapped in Syria would have come about only after the deployment of an approximately 100,000-strong contingent of US/international ground troops to overthrow Assad. As was also mentioned, neither the US government (pre- or post-2016) nor any other member of the international community seriously contemplated taking on such a massive engagement to bring about such an outcome.

When it comes to the US response to the Khan Shaykhun chemical attacks, we need to acknowledge that in essence, Trump decided to prioritize this action's retaliatory character over the humanitarian needs of saving the lives of people who were still very much in danger. Nevertheless, even the decision to intervene was taken in the aftermath of specific humanitarian considerations. The question remains how we had arrived at that situation. In this respect, it is good to start by stating that the United Nations decides whether to intervene in any given country. Naturally, as far as international law is concerned, the Security Council is solely responsible for sanctioning coercion in the global environment and has a comprehensive mandate to decide what measures should be taken to restore the rule of law in the conflict zones of the contemporary world.

Naturally, this can be manifested in the protection and promotion of human rights, the condemnation of rogue regimes for the mistreatment of civilian populations, the authorization to use force to restore the status quo, or humanitarian intervention or any other form of peacekeeping missions in regions where an armed conflict has ceased and the presence of an international contingent is required to secure enforcement of peace treaties, disarmament, demobilization, or any further reintegration of former combatants. Also, regardless of whether the system that we adopted in 1945 can prevent countries from waging wars, we have not managed to develop an internationally recognized norm permitting the use of state force to stop other states from killing or expelling their people. The need to further recognize and institutionalize this concept brought the United Nations (UN) to life. Nevertheless, despite this system's complexity and our legislation's strength, we still suffer from a lack of the ability to use clearly defined retaliatory measures against those who violate international law. This naturally opens up the question of protecting fundamental human rights and analyzing the situations in which they are so openly violated.

Other questions remain, such as whether it is moral to be an onlooker who sits idle and observes what is going on in Syria or any other similar regional conflict. Do we expect that these conflicts will resolve themselves at their own pace? It seems that it is high time to end these hostilities, but the involved sides still do not want to acknowledge it. Once they stop fighting, the question will inevitably arise: will the international community be ready to offer the Syrian people a Marshall plan that will allow them to rebuild their country? Does it mean that since there are no reasonable answers to these questions, we as humans are slowly but steadily descending a slippery slope? To answer these questions, it is advisable to look into the debate in question through the Just War Theory (jus bellum) that, by extension, has been too vigorous for the last few centuries.

There are several existing international rules and regulations that can provide justification or reasons to go to war (*jus ad bellum*) and govern how warfare is conducted during war (*jus in bello*), and there is also a concept that deals with the norms that should be followed after any conflict is terminated (*jus post-bellum*), which provides many general rules and regulations related to rebuilding in post-conflict zones.

To start deliberations on the possibility of any humanitarian intervention in Syria at any stage of this conflict, we need to clarify that its likelihood was rather minimal from the beginning. This became clear not only because of the monumental 2008 economic crisis but also because the US government had been deeply involved in its operations in Afghanistan and Iraq. The massive detriment to the US's reputation during G. W. Bush's two terms was steadily reversed during Obama's years in power, but the episodes mentioned above taught Washington insiders that the US was not as invincible as had been commonly believed. For any humanitarian action of a Western-style to happen, it would have to have had the US's stamp of approval, but there was simply no appetite for such an action. At the beginning of the uprising in 2011, the general opinion was that even if they behaved as the most genuine humanitarian power, no humanitarian intervention in Syria could happen with American boots on the ground. Therefore, Obama was cautious not to make the same mistakes as his predecessor, and he knew that engaging in Syria may have turned out very counterproductively both for Syria and the US since such an action would not have been welcomed by most of the parties involved in the conflict.

Hypothetically, if such an intervention had happened, Assad would have gained a handy excuse to present it as an American/Western or imperialist attempt to meddle in Syrian affairs. Meanwhile, some of the moderate rebels involved in the confrontation against the Syrian regime would have mistrusted the White House's intentions, for such an action could have been seen as an instrumental attempt to take over and solve their problems in a way that they would have lost control over. Naturally, had the countries in Syria's vicinity decided to intervene on a humanitarian basis, it would have been a completely different story. Such a region-based intervention could have achieved most of its short- and medium-term objectives at a relatively lower cost. Nevertheless, there was very little political will to organize such a collective intervention in the regional capitals.

Michael Walzer's work and the Ghouta attacks

I have recently approached the background of the situation in Syria after the Ghouta attacks, through a Walzerian lens, and I need to admit that I generally agree with his intake on the situation in question for Michael Walzer was more than convinced that the Syrian regime was behind these attacks and yet he still decided to advocate in favor of a far-reaching restraint in respect of any potential retaliation against Assad that had been suggested by other political commentators at that time. I agree with the suggestion, outlined in the commentary for *Dissent Magazine* before these attacks (May 14, 2013), where Walzer suggested that Obama's 2012 speech that declared a ban on the use of chemical weapons in Syria must have contributed to a change in the dynamics of the Syria debate between those who believed that the U.S. government had an obligation to intervene to defend President Obama's red lines and those who advocated restraint. I strongly believe that the Ghouta attacks created a good reason for both U.N.-led intervention and a collective defense action, an exception from the rules and principles protecting the state sovereignty of the state perpetrator of this action.

Walzer also thought that however scandalous alleged Assad loyalists' actions were and however far-reaching Obama's anti-chemical weapons declaration was, the U.S. government had no moral or legal obligation to act unilaterally to punish the Syrian regime for its actions, suggesting that it was advisable to rely on the old good maxim "anyone who can, should", as, from his perspective, no one can be forced to take responsibility for intervening if they are unwilling to do so. He reiterated that no one should expect the U.S. to intervene wherever human rights are violated. This is a very strong argument, that the international community should seriously consider similar situations, instead of relying solely on the decision of one country.

His later commentary for *Dissent Magazine* (October 30, 2013), was also very convincing for Walzer suggested in this piece that "America is not the cause of this human disaster. We stayed out of Syria, but that didn't help the Syrians. I think that it is now morally necessary to ask: What if we hadn't stayed out? Might we in this case (every case is different) have avoided or mitigated the disaster?" This scholar also emphasized that by standing on the sidelines and negotiating with the Russian diplomats the best possible course was achieved for the broader Syrian people's safety has been achieved. As he pointed out, in the end, this imperfect diplomatic solution resulted in Syria's voluntary removal of a large proportion of its chemical weapons stockpiles, and this was possible only thanks to the U.S. threat to attack Syria.

Subsequently, in an interview with Alex Stark (September 10, 2013), Walzer clarified that from his perspective, it would be criminally insane not to attempt to stop chemicals from landing in the wrong hands. The attempt to coerce the Syrian regime to comply with an international body established to dismantle its chemical weapons was the only positive outcome that offered a far greater payoff than strikes on Syrian authorities could have achieved. As he suggested, even if the Syrian leader's cooperation came at the price of the promise of no military retaliation against his regime, the Russian-U.S. agreement on the destruction and dismantling of Syrian chemical weapons did not include bringing responsible parties to justice.

It is not ideal that those responsible for these deadly attacks went unpunished, but Walzer was not willing to question these arrangements and he was right about it, for they seemed to be perfectly suited to the situation. For him, Obama's decision in response to the Ghouta attacks was perfectly rational, for the circumstances on the ground made any humanitarian intervention impossible, which is why he also suggested launching a new debate on Syria without subjecting the involved parties to self-referential moralizing and anti-moralizing arguments that had put a strain on the discussion.

Further Discussion

The Syrian conflict has caused catastrophic casualties, one of the worst humanitarian disasters in the 21st century, damage to the local economy, trade, and industry, the destruction of resources and the human base, and the tragedy of more than 12 million refugees and internally displaced people. The ultimate responsibility for the cataclysm of this senseless war lies on the shoulders of not only the regime, the opposition forces, and the jihadists, but is also shared with their foreign handlers who support them from afar, either by sending arms and ammunition or providing the diplomatic coverage for specific actions on the ground.

That being said, it has been proven beyond a reasonable doubt that in this particular instance, Assad and his loyalists were directly responsible for orchestrating the Ghouta chemical attacks of 21 August 2013. Effectively, in its direct aftermath, the P5 members came together and began working on a more tangible way to deal with the deteriorating situation on the ground in Syria. There were also a series of US-Russia bilateral meetings in which they came up with the so-called Lavrov-Kerry plan that sanctioned an unwritten agreement that if he would hand over all of the chemical agents Syria had in its arsenal, the international community would not prosecute Assad for the crimes committed in August 2013.

The paradox of this situation is that the Ghouta attacks could have justified a humanitarian intervention in Syria on a military basis as it was certain that the Assad regime used these prohibited weapons against his political opponents and fellow citizens. But in the end, Obama decided not to pursue any unilateral retaliatory actions against the culprits of this international crime. In fact, this outcome was secured thanks to the Russian foreign minister's intervention at the last moment, as Lavrov managed to persuade the Syrian government to hand over their chemical weapons stockpiles to international authorities. The logic behind this action can be explained by the need for the removal of these deadly weapons from the Syrian theater of war so they would not end up in the wrong hands of a less predictable government. The application of this logic was heavily criticized, especially given the fact that it was reported that the Assad regime has used chemical weapons on several occasions after 2013 (Bandeira & Alberto 2019; Human Rights Watch 2013).

Effectively, instead of punishing one of the biggest human rights abusers in the region, Assad's rule was artificially extended, which happened at the expense of Syrian society at large. Under normal circumstances. hiding behind the protective shield of state sovereignty when a regime commits appalling atrocities should not be allowed, at least as far as the Responsibility to Protect Doctrine is concerned, but the members of the international community have proven to be very reluctant to chase such individuals as Bashar al-Assad to "the gates of hell" to bring them to justice. On the contrary, the Assad example illustrates that even if you are a human rights violator when you have such powerful friends as Russia and President Putin who seem to be inclined to protect your interest no matter what, you can basically sleep tight, as nothing bad is going to happen to you. If it had not been for Putin, the Syrian leader would most probably have attempted to flee his country in the manner of Ukrainian President Victor Yanukovych, who fled Ukraine in 2014, as he would have been afraid of facing the same fate as Muammar Gadhafi and Saddam Hussein. However, Assad did not have to "worry too much" about his personal safety and his political future, for Russia had blocked every UNSC suggestion of the necessity of the implementation of the so-called collective self-defense action of the former Yugoslavia type (Prendergast 2019; Ruthven 2014).

That being said, it would also be very naïve to expect that each and every P5 member state would restrain themselves from prioritizing their national interests in order to meet their global responsibilities, so I agree with Michael Waltz that Barack Obama was right to embrace the outcome of the bilateral negotiations with Russia regarding the casus of Syria in good faith, outside the UNSC decision-making table. It was not a cynical decision, it was a good decision, even though soon afterward, Syria became the site of a number of regime chemical attacks, at least their scale was more manageable. Ultimately, thanks to Obama's decision, much larger humanitarian disasters in the making were averted as tons of chemical weapons did not end up in the hands of Abu Bakr al-Baghdadi or other radicals from ISIS or al-Nusra.

Still, we need to acknowledge a clear limitation of our UN-based global security system, for when it comes to human rights protection initiatives, international law, and the way the UN collective global security system has been arranged, it seems that international legislators have put too much emphasis on developing a very comprehensive set of laws and regulations preventing countries from waging wars against each other and protecting the state sovereignty of any given country, but too little has been done to create conditions to protect the human rights of endangered populations in civil war scenarios.

Even though the story of the Syrian conflict and the international community's response to the use of prohibited chemical weapons has no happy ending, the UN-based collective security system is not a dysfunctional relic of the past, for there is a way to change it either through evolution or revolution, and we can learn a very valuable lesson from our policy-making mistakes in Syria.

Disclaimer

This manuscript was completed before the outbreak of Russia's War in Ukraine in 2022. Therefore, it does not offer a more comprehensive level of analysis that would have compared the situation in both war zones. However, it still can be used as a helpful point of reference in a broader debate on the scope and scale of the international community's responsibility to bring peace and security back to the contemporary conflict zone affected by hypothetical chemical weapons attacks. Given that Putin's war in Ukraine does not look like a victorious campaign by any standard of imagination, and considering that the international community had shown a far-reaching restraint when it comes to bringing the regimes that directly benefited from the use of chemical weapons to justice, we can make an educated guess that President of Russian Federation and the commanders under his command may have the incentive to resort to the weapons of mass destruction to pursue particular military objectives if their army continues to underperform. Unfortunately, it is doubtful that Russia would not be discouraged by any crossing-the-red-line-type-of-rhetoric that threatens this country or its officials with some severe consequences in the

event of any use of chemical weapons in Ukraine,
for Putin still sees them as empty threats.

Bibliography

ACAPS. 2022. "Boko Haram in Chad." https://www.acaps.org/country/chad/crisis/bok o-haram-

Armament Research Services (ARES) "Chemical Weapons Attack in Eastern Ghouta, Syria. A Visual Summary of an Open-Source Investigation." Human Rights Center, UC Berkeley School of Law. October 7, 2020. https://storymaps.arcgis.com/stories/56c19f1d bcbb4054b524cacc5f6a9fa5.

ANYADIKE, Obi. 2022. "When peace comes: Imagining the end of Nigeria's Boko Haram war." https://www.thenewhumanitarian.org/feature/2 022/1/20/peace-young-nigerians-imagine-end-of-Boko-Haram-war.

BAKER, Peter; WEISMAN, Jonathan; STACK, Liam; MURPHY, Heather. 2013. "What to watch for in Obama's speech" Originally published September 10, 2013, at 5:55 pm Updated September 11, 2013, at 5:44 am. https://www.seattletimes.com/nation-world/what-to-watch-for-in-obamarsquos-speech/.

BALANCHE, Fabrice. 2021. "The Assad Regime Has Failed to Restore Full Sovereignty Over Syria." The Washington Institute for Near East Policy. Feb 10, 2021. https://www.washingtoninstitute.org/policy-analysis/assad-regime-has-failed-restore-full-sovereignty-over-syria.

BALOCH, Shah Meer. 2022. "'We are happy to fight you': tensions rise on Afghan-Pakistani border" Wed 9 Feb 2022. https://www.theguardian.com/world/2022/feb/09/we-are-happy-to-fight-deadly-tension-on-the-afghanistan-pakistan-border-taliban.

BBC Report. 2018. "Russia says 63,000 troops have seen combat in Syria," 23 August 2018. https://www.bbc.com/news/world-middle-east-45284121.

BORGER, Julian. 2013. Syrian chemical attack used sarin and was worst in 25 years, says UN. Tue 17 Sep 2013 08.25 BST. https://www.theguardian.com/world/2013/sep/16/syrian-chemical-attack-sarin-says-un.

BRZEZINSKI, Zbigniew. 2007. Second Chance: Three Presidents and the Crisis of American Superpower. New York: Basic Books.

BURKE, Joseph. 2017. The Responsibility to Protect and the Syrian Civil War. Human Rights LL.M. Thesis. Supervisor: Marjan Ajevski, Dr. Central European University.

CHAPPELL, Bill. 2014. "ISIS Declares Caliphate
    as Iraq Fights to Retake Tikrit" 30th June
    2014. https://www.npr.org/sections/thetwo-
    way/2014/06/30/326905464/isis-declares-
    caliphate-as-iraq-fights-to-retake-tikrit.

CHEMICAL WEAPONS ATTACK IN
    EASTERN GHOUTA, Syria. A Visual
    Summary of an Open-Source Investigation".
    Human Rights Center, UC Berkeley School of
    Law. October 7, 2020.
    https://storymaps.arcgis.com/stories/56c19f1d
    bcbb4054b524cacc5f6a9fa5.

CHISHTI, Ali K. 2014. "Al Qaeda 'retreating' in
    Pakistan." DW. Date 08.12.2014.

COMOLLI, Virginia. 2017. "The evolution and
    impact of Boko Haram in the Lake Chad
    Basin" October 2017.
    https://odihpn.org/magazine/the-evolution-
    and-impact-of-boko-haram-in-the-lake-chad-
    basin.

CHULOV, Martin; MAHMOOD, Mona;
    SAMPLE, Ian. 2013. "Syria conflict: chemical
    weapons blamed as hundreds reported killed"
    https://www.theguardian.com/world/2013/aug/
    21/syria-conflcit-chemical-weapons-hundreds-
    killed.

CURIEL, Rafael Prieto; WALTHER, Olivier; O'CLERY, Neave. 2020. "Uncovering the internal structure of Boko Haram through its mobility patterns," Applied Network Science. https://appliednetsci.springeropen.com/articles/10.1007/s41109-020-00264-4.

DAVISON, Derek. 2018. "Interview with Joshua Landis: What Happens Now in Syria?" June 19, 2018 https://lobelog.com/author/derek-davison.

DAHER, Joseph. 2018. "Three Years Later: The Evolution of Russia's Military Intervention In Syria", September 27, 2018. https://www.atlanticcouncil.org/blogs/syriasource/three-years-later-the-evolution-of-russia-s-military-intervention-in-syria.

GARTENSTEIN-ROSS, Daveed, et al., "Islamic State Vs. Al-Qaeda: Strategic Dimensions of a Patricidal Conflict," New America, December 2015, https://static.newamerica.org/attachments/12103-islamic-state-vs-al-qaeda/ISISvAQ_Final.e68fdd22a90e49c4af1d4cd0dc9e3651.pdf.

DEARDEN, Lizzie. ISIS Calls on Women to Fight and Launch Terror Attacks for the First Time. Independent, 6 October. 2017.

DEARDEN, Lizzie. ISIS Propaganda Video
Shows Women Fighting for the First Time
Amid Desperation to Bolster Ranks.
Independent, 8 Feb. 2018.

WASHINGTON POST'S EDITORIAL BOARD
(2020), "Opinion: Syria's brutal dictatorship
suffers a severe setback,"
https://www.washingtonpost.com/opinions/glo
bal-opinions/syrias-brutal-dictatorship-suffers-
a-severe-setback/2020/06/23/355548ac-b0c0-
11ea-8f56-63f38c990077_story.html.

EIZENGA, Daniel. 2021. "Chad's Escalating Fight
against Boko Haram." African Center for
Strategic Studies.
https://africacenter.org/spotlight/chad-
escalating-fight-against-boko-haram.

Final Documents of the CWC Review Conference
of the CWC review conference for 2013, 2008,
and 2003"
https://www.un.org/disarmament/wmd/chemic
al.

GARDNER, Frank. 2015. "The crucial role of
women within Islamic State." 20 August 2015.
https://www.bbc.com/news/world-middle-east-
33985441.

GARDNER, Frank. 2014. "'Jihadistan': Can Isis
militants rule seized territory?"
https://www.bbc.com/news/world-middle-east-
28222872.

GENSER, Jared, and I. COTLER. 2012. The responsibility to protect: the promise of stopping mass atrocities in our time. Oxford: Oxford University Press.

GUL, Ayaz. 2022. "Pakistan Vows to Continue Fencing Afghan Border, Downplays Taliban Disruptive Acts." January 03, 2022, 12:11. https://www.voanews.com/a/pakistan-vows-to-continue-fencing-afghan-border-downplays-taliban-disruptive-acts-/6379947.html.

HASSAN, Hassan. 2013. "How the Muslim Brotherhood Hijacked Syria's Revolution. The shadowy Islamist group that was all but destroyed in the 1980s is ruining the uprising against Bashar al-Assad". March 13, 2013, 3:12 PM. www.foreignpolicy.com/2013/03/13/how-the-muslim-brotherhood-hijacked-syrias-revolution.

HASSAN, Mohammed. 2020. "How ISIS Is Restructuring and Repositioning." Chatham House: Analysis. February 2020. https://syria.chathamhouse.org/research/how-isis-is-restructuring-and-repositioning.

HIGGINS, Eliot. 2014. "Identifying Government Positions During the August 21st Sarin Attacks." July 15, 2014. https://www.bellingcat.com/news/mena/2014/07/15/identifying-government-positions-during-the-august-21st-sarin-attacks.

Human Rights Watch. (Organization). 2021. Report from Nairobi "Cameroon: Boko Haram Attacks Escalate in Far North," https://www.hrw.org/news/2021/04/05/camero on-boko-haram-attacks-escalate-far-north.

HUMAN RIGHTS WATCH. (Organization). 2017. Flawed justice: accountability for ISIS crimes in Iraq. https://www.hrw.org/report/2017/12/05/flawed -justice/accountability-isis-crimes-iraq.

Human Rights Watch. (Organization). 2015. "Syria: Stories Behind Photos of Killed Detainees Caesar Photos' Victims Identified." https://www.hrw.org/news/2015/12/16/syria- stories-behind-photos-killed-detainees.

HUMAN RIGHTS WATCH. (Organization). 2013. Attacks on Ghouta: analysis of alleged use of chemical weapons in Syria. New York: Human Rights Watch. https://www.hrw.org/sites/default/files/reports/ syria_cw0913_web_1.pdf.

IANS, "Taliban active in Pakistan too, retain links with Al Qaeda." https://www.msn.com/en- in/news/world/taliban-active-in-pakistan-too- retain-links-with-al-qaeda/ar-AAMed21.

ISMAIL, Salwa. (2011). "The Syrian Uprising: Imagining and Performing the Nation". Studies in Ethnicity and Nationalism: Vol. 11, No. 3.

KHATIB, Lina. 2019. "Abu Bakr al-Baghdadi: What His Death Means for ISIS in Syria." Expert Comment. 28 October 2019. Chatham House. https://www.chathamhouse.org/2019/10/abu-bakr-al-baghdadi-what-his-death-means-isis-syria.

KINDZEKA, Moki Edwin. 2021. "Cameroon Says Boko Haram Attacks Military, Seduces Civilians" July 30, 2021, 8:09 AM. https://www.voanews.com/a/africa_cameroon-says-boko-haram-attacks-military-seduces-civilians/6208936.html.

KUGELMAN, Michael. 2022. "The Taliban Pick Fight Over Border with Pakistan." January 6, 2022, 5:00 PM. https://foreignpolicy.com/2022/01/06/taliban-pakistan-afghanistan-border-fight/.

LANDIS, Joshua. 2012. "The Syrian Uprising of 2011: Why the Assad Regime Is Likely to Survive to 2013", Middle East Policy, Vol. XIX, No. 1, Spring 2012.

MIR, Asfandyar; OLSON, Richard; WATKINS, Andrew. 2022. "Afghanistan-Pakistan Border Dispute Heats Up. Taliban's repudiation of Pakistan's position on the Durand Line challenges a pillar of Pakistan's security policy." January 12, 2022. https://www.usip.org/publications/2022/01/afghanistan-pakistan-border-dispute-heats.

"Pakistan Launches Al Qaeda Sweep." https://edition.cnn.com/2004/WORLD/asiapcf/02/23/pakistan.alqaeda/index.html.

PIETRZAK, Piotr. 2021a. *On the Idea of Humanitarian Intervention. A New Compartmentalization of IR Theories.* New York: Columbia University Press. https://cup.columbia.edu/book/on-the-idea-of-humanitarian-intervention/9783838215921.

PIETRZAK, Piotr. 2021b. "Immanuel Kant and Niccolò Machiavelli's traditions and the limits of approaching contemporary conflicts -the case study of the Syrian Conflict (2011-present)" In In Statu Nascendi Journal of Political Philosophy and International Relations 2021/2, p. 53–84.

PIETRZAK, Piotr. 2019a. "On Human Rights in Syria: Deliberations on the universality of Human Rights and the International Community's Reaction to the Syrian conflict (2011 - 2019)" in *Сборник "Универсалност и приложимост на човешките права".* Edited by Veselin Hristov Dafov, Ivan Kirkov, Tsena Zhelyazkova, Sofia 2020, ISBN: 978-954-07-4989-1, Pages: 152.

PIETRZAK, Piotr. 2019b. "The Syrian Conflict (2011–ongoing): How a Perfectly Winnable Uprising Has Ended Up as a Ferocious Proxy War of Global Importance". In: In Statu Nascendi Journal of Political Philosophy and International Relations 2019/1, p. 34–98. https://cup.columbia.edu/book/in-statu-nascendi/9783838213095.

PIETRZAK, Piotr. 2018. "Kremlin's Reaction to the St. Petersburg Metro Attacks seen through the Prism of Russian Intervention in Syria", In *In Statu Nascendi Journal of Political Philosophy and International Relations* 2018/1, p. 101 – 116.

PIETRZAK, Piotr. 2018. "The Short, Medium and Long-Term Implications of the Russian Intervention in Syria (2015 - 2019)", *International Scientific Conference Security, Political and Legal Challenges of the Modern World,*

PIETRZAK, Piotr. 2013. "The United Nations Security Council voting on the draft resolution S/2012/77 and the prospects for a humanitarian intervention in Syria seen through the prism of the Realist and the Liberal schools of the International Relations Theory", a Dissertation written under the supervision of Prof. Yoram Gorlizki, the Manchester University, submitted to the University of Manchester for the degree of Master of Arts. Deposited at Manchester University Library in 2013.

PRENDERGAST, Molly. 2019. "Madonnas and whores or blood and gore? Roles for women in the so-called Islamic State." *In Statu Nascendi: Journal of Political Philosophy and International Relations* 2019/2. p. 3 – 36.

REISMAN, W. Michael; STEVICK, Douglas L. "The Applicability of International Law Standards to United Nations Economic Sanctions Programmes," European Journal of International Law, Volume 9, Issue 1, 1998, Pages 86–141, https://doi.org/10.1093/ejil/9.1.86.

CIVIL RIGHTS DEFENDERS et al. 2013. Report on eastern and western Ghouta sarin attack. https://crd.org/wp-content/uploads/2021/04/EASTERN-GHOUTA-SUMMARY-EN-final.pdf.

RICHINICK, Michele. 2013. "Obama: I didn't set a red line, the world set a red line". MSNBC. 09/04/13 11:00 AM. Updated 10/24/13, 10:16 AM. Available at:<http://www.msnbc.com/morning-joe/obama-i-didnt-set-red-line-the- world.

ROGGIO, Bill. 2006. "The Pakistani Frontier." https://www.longwarjournal.org/archives/2006/01/the_pakistani_fronti.php.

"Syria Chemical Attack: What We Know." https://www.bbc.com/news/world-middle-east-23927399.

SAYED, Abdul. 2020. "The Future of al-Qaeda in Afghanistan & Pakistan." https://newlinesinstitute.org/al-qaeda/the-future-of-al-qaeda-in-afghanistan-pakistan.

SHAOUL, Jean. 2014. "Reports reveal the scale of destruction of Syria's world historic heritage." 29 December 2014. https://www.wsws.org/en/articles/2014/12/29/syri-d29.html.

STARK. A. 2013, September 10. Interview - Michael Walzer. E-International Relations. Retrieved December 27, 2022, from https://www.e-ir.info/2013/09/10/interview-michael-walzer.

WALZER, Michael. 2013, October 30. "Were We Wrong about Syria?" *Dissent Magazine.* Retrieved December 27, 2022, from https://www.dissentmagazine.org/blog/were-we-wrong-about-syria.

WALZER, Michael. 2013, May 13. "Syria: What Ought to be Done?" - *Dissent Magazine.* Retrieved December 26, 2022, from https://www.dissentmagazine.org/blog/syria-what-ought-to-be-done.

WALZER, Michael. 2012. "The Aftermath of War." In *Ethics Beyond War's End, ed. E. Patterson*, 35-46. Georgetown: Georgetown University Press.

WALZER, Michael. 2012, March 9. "Syria" - *Dissent Magazine.* Retrieved December 26, 2022, from https://www.dissentmagazine.org/blog/syria.

WALZER, Michael. 2011, March 20. "The Case Against Our Attack on Libya." The Case Against Our Attack on Libya. *the New Republic.* Retrieved December 27, 2022, from https://newrepublic.com/article/85509/the-case-against-our-attack-libya.

TAYO, Teniola. 2022. "Analysis: How Boko
    Haram, Lake Chad Basin's security dilemmas
    can be tackled," Institute for Security Studies.
    January 24, 2022.
    https://www.premiumtimesng.com/features-
    and-interviews/507555-analysis-how-boko-
    haram-lake-chad-basins-security-dilemmas-
    can-be-tackled.html.

Ramesh THAKUR and William MALEY (eds.).
    2015. Theorising the Responsibility to Protect,
    Cambridge University Press, Cambridge.

SLINGER, John. 2013. "It is not enough for the
    west to punish Syria's use of chemical
    weapons alone". 29 August 2013.
    http://www.newstatesman.com/politics/2013/0
    8/it-not-enough-west-punish-syrias-use-
    chemical-weapons-alone.

SEVEN, Ümit. 2022. Russia's Foreign Policy
    Actions and the Syrian Civil War in the United
    Nations Security Council, Journal of Balkan
    and Near Eastern Studies, DOI:
    10.1080/19448953.2022.2037966.

The General Assembly of the National Coalition of
     Syrian Revolution and Opposition Forces "The
     Chemical Weapons Dossier and the US -
     Russia Agreement. - September 15, 2013".
     Final Statement 9th Istanbul, Turkey.
     September 16, 2013.
     http://en.etilaf.org/press/the-general-assembly-
     of-the-national-coalition-of-syrian-revolution-
     and-opposition-forces-september-15-
     2013.html.

The Organization for The Prohibition of Chemical
     Weapons (OPCW). 2013. "Destruction of
     Syrian Chemical Weapons".
     https://www.opcw.org/sites/default/files/docu
     ments/EC/M-33/ecm33dec01_e_.pdf.

UNICEF. 2022. "Boko Haram Crisis,"
     https://www.unicefusa.org/mission/emergencie
     s/conflict/boko-haram-crisis.

United States, and Bill Clinton. 1998. Report
     regarding peacekeeping efforts in Former
     Yugoslavia: communication from the
     President of the United States transmitting a
     supplemental report consistent with the War
     Powers Resolution, on U.S. contributions in
     support of peacekeeping efforts in the Former
     Yugoslavia. Washington: U.S. G.P.O.

U.S. Mission in Geneva. 2013. Secretary of State Kerry and Russian Foreign Minister Lavrov press remarks after their meeting." September 14, 2013. https://geneva.usmission.gov/2013/09/14/transcript-secretary-of-state-kerry-and-russian-foreign-minister-lavrov-press-remarks-after-their-meeting.

U.S. Response to the Reported Chemical Attack in Douma, Syria | Center for Strategic and International Studies (csis.org).

VASINA, James; NOAH, Stéphane; SCHIEX, Erwan; MENGA, Tony Michael; NSONO, Claudia. 2021. "Former Boko Haram jihadists get a second chance in Cameroon," Issued on: 16/09/2021 - 16:59. Modified: 16/09/2021 - 17:08. https://www.france24.com/en/tv-shows/focus/20210916-former-boko-haram-jihadists-get-second-chance-in-cameroon.

WALT, Stephen M. 2015. "What Should We Do if the Islamic State Wins?" (10/06/2015) *Foreign Policy Magazine*. https://foreignpolicy.com/2015/06/10/what-should-we-do-if-isis-islamic-state-wins-containment.

 **PIOTR PIETRZAK, Ph.D** specializes in the Middle East & the Islamic World; he looks at his research area through the prism of some of the most exciting developments in International Relations theory, geopolitics, conflict resolution strategies, and international law. His primary interests relate to relatively recent socio-political developments in Afghanistan, Cyprus, Chechnya, the Former Yugoslavia, Iraq, Iran, Syria, Egypt, Mali, Georgia, and Ukraine.

Pietrzak is also a co-founder and an editor-in-chief of *In Statu Nascendi – Journal of Political Philosophy and International Relations**, a non-profit charitable organization based in Sofia, Bulgaria. He holds a Ph.D. Degree in Philosophy from **Sofia University St. Kliment Ohridiski** (2021), a master's degree in International Politics & International Relations from **the University of Manchester** (2013), and a Master's Degree in Politics from **the University of Warmia and Mazury** (2008). He was awarded an Erasmus Scholarship to **the University of Cyprus** in 2007.

For more information in respect of the **Ghouta Chemical Attack** and the international community's response to this blatant example of human rights abuse, please See: Pietrzak, Piotr. 2022. *On the Idea of Humanitarian Intervention - A New Compartmentalization of IR Theories*. [S.L.]: Ibidem-Verlag. P. 155-178. In this publication, I challenge the preconceived notions about humanitarian intervention and discuss its hypothetical implementation in Syria through the prism of the broader international perspective.

Selected Work of the Author

Pietrzak, Piotr. [Forthcoming in 2023]. *The Brzezinski Doctrine and NATO's Response to Russia's Assault on Ukraine,*

Pietrzak, Piotr. [Forthcoming in 2023]. "Integrating Ontology *in statu nascendi* in the main currents of International Relations Theory." *In Statu Nascendi – Journal of Political Philosophy and International Relations* Vol. 6, No. 1 2023,

Pietrzak, Piotr. 2023. "Michael Walzer's work and the idea of humanitarian intervention in Syria (2011-present): The International Response to the Situation in Syria During and after the Arab Spring in *Interdisciplinary Approaches to the Regulation of the Modern Global Migration and Economic Crisis*. Edited by Alaverdov, Emilia, and Muhammad Waseem Bari. 2023, DOI: 10.4018/978-1-6684-6334-5.

Pietrzak, Piotr. "The International Community's
     Response to the Putinization of the Situation in
     Ukraine." *Modern Diplomacy*, December 22, 2022.
     https://moderndiplomacy.eu/2022/12/22/the-
     international-communitys-response-to-the-
     putinization-of-the-situation-in-ukraine/.

Pietrzak, Piotr. 2022. "The International Community's
     Response to the Ghouta Chemical Attack of 2013"
     - *Acta Politica Polonica* 2/2022 (54) -
     Wydawnictwo Naukowe Uniwersytetu
     Szczecińskiego, January 1, 2022.
     https://wnus.edu.pl/ap/en/issue/1253/article/19956/
     .

Pietrzak, Piotr. 2022. "Introducing the idea of Ontology
     in statu nascendi to the broader International
     Relations Theory" *International Conference
     Proceeding Series - International Conference on
     Economics and Social Sciences in Serik*, Turkey on
     21 - 23 Oct 2022.
     https://www.eclss.org/publicationsfordoi/abst11act
     8boo8kIE%26SS2022_antalya.pdf,

Pietrzak, Piotr. 2023. "Michael Walzer's work and the
     idea of humanitarian intervention in Syria (2011-
     present)," in *Interdisciplinary Approaches to the
     Regulation of the Modern Global Migration and
     Economic Crisis*. Edited by Alaverdov, Emilia, and
     Muhammad Waseem Bari. 2023.
     https://eclss.org/publicationsfordoi/prGrm_E&SS2
     022_merged.pdf,

Пиетшак, Пьотр. Балканският полуостров „in statu nascendi" и защо понятието „балканизация" не е вече адекватно? / Пьотр Пиетшак. // *Международни отношения*, LI, 2022, N 2, 59-64.

Pietrzak, Piotr. 2022. "A Comparative Study of Russia's War in Ukraine (2014-, including its 2022 escalation), Russia's aggression in Georgia (2008), and Russia's Military Operations in Syria (2015-)" *International Conference Proceeding Series - VII. International Middle East Symposium: Political and Social Stability in the Middle East* (May 10-11th, 2022, Online) http://acikerisim.gelisim.edu.tr/xmlui/handle/1136 3/3724?show=full,

Pietrzak, Piotr. 2022. "The Putinization of the situation of women and children during the 2022 Russian invasion of Ukraine" *In Statu Nascendi Vol. 5, No. 2 (2022) Journal of Political Philosophy and International Relations: Special Issue: Gender Equality in Politics and International Relations,* pp. 19-76.

Pietrzak, Piotr. 2022. "How did Bashar Al-Assad Get Away with the Ghouta Chemical Attack?: The Promise of Relinquishing Syria's Chemical Weapons Arsenal that was Never Fully Fulfilled," in *Regulating human rights, social security, and socio-economic structures in a global perspective.* Edited by Alaverdov, Emilia, and Muhammad Waseem Bari. 2022, DOI: 10.4018/978-1-6684-4620-1.ch008.

Pietrzak, Piotr. 2021. *On the idea of humanitarian intervention: a new compartmentalization of IR theories*, Ibidem Verlag: Stuttgart, 2021

Pietrzak, Piotr. 2019. "The Syrian Conflict (2011–ongoing): How a Perfectly Winnable Uprising has been transformed into a Civil War, Only to End up as a Ferocious Proxy War of Global Importance," *In Statu Nascendi – Journal of Political Philosophy and International Relations* Vol. 2, No. 1 2019, p. 34–95, ISBN: 9783838213095,

Interviews

Pietrzak, Piotr & Żęgota, Krzysztof .2021: "Interview with Krzysztof Żęgota, PhD on the Russian Federation's Geostrategic Imperatives and Vladimir Putin's future." *In Statu Nascendi – Journal of Political Philosophy and International Relations* Vol. 4, No. 1 (2021),

Albertini, Tamara & Pietrzak, Piotr. 2020. "Clarity is what I seek first: A scientific interview with Professor Tamara Albertini by Piotr Pietrzak," *In Statu Nascendi – Journal of Political Philosophy and International Relations* Vol. 3, No. 2 (2020), p. 3–18, ISBN: 9783838214290,

Kojcic, Zoran & Pietrzak, Piotr. 2020. "Interview with Dr. Zoran Kojcic", *In Statu Nascendi – Journal of Political Philosophy and International Relations* Vol. 3, No. 1 (2020), p. 85–92, ISBN: 9783838214290,

Mehmeti, Sami & Pietrzak, Piotr. 2020. "Interview with Dr. Sami Mehmeti on the political situation in North Macedonia & Balkans in statu nascendi,", *In Statu Nascendi – Journal of Political Philosophy and International Relations* Vol. 2, No. 2 (2019), p. 109–116, ISBN: 9783838213392,

Dimitrova, Maria & Pietrzak, Piotr. 2019. "Interview with Prof. Maria Dimitrova on Emmanuel Levinas' Philosophy," *In Statu Nascendi – Journal of Political Philosophy and International Relations* Vol. 2, No. 1 (2019), p. 177–185, ISBN: 9783838213095,

Grabowski, Marcin & Pietrzak, Piotr. 2019. "Interview with Marcin Grabowski, Ph.D., on the Ever-Changing Political Situation of the Asia Pacific Region in General, and the Political Backdrop of North Korea in Particular," *In Statu Nascendi – Journal of Political Philosophy and International Relations* Vol. 2, No. 1 (2019), p. 3–32, ISBN: 9783838213095,

Pietrzak, Piotr & Trupia, Francesco. 2018. "Interview with Francesco Trupia on the Nagorno-Karabakh Conflict,", In Statu Nascendi – *Journal of Political Philosophy and International Relations* Vol 1, No 1, (2018), p. 117–128, ISBN: 9783838212296,

Book reviews

Pietrzak, Piotr. 2020. "A brief introduction to the Journal of Romanian Studies, Vol. 1, No. 1 (2019)." In Statu Nascendi – *Journal of Political Philosophy and International Relations* Vol. 3, No. 2 (2020), p. 156–158, ISBN: 9783838214696,

Pietrzak, Piotr. 2018. "Chapter Review:
    Disenchantment and Re-enchantment: Chapter 3,
    The death of God and the Crisis of Philosophy.
    Neascu, Michaela. (2010) *Hans J. Morgenthau's
    Theory of International Relations*," *In Statu
    Nascendi – Journal of Political Philosophy and
    International Relations* Vol 1, No 1, (2018), p. 77–
    81, ISBN: 9783838212296,

Pietrzak, Piotr. 2018. György Lukács: "The young
    Hegel: Studies in the Relations between Dialectics
    and Economics," *In Statu Nascendi – Journal of
    Political Philosophy and International Relations*
    Vol 1, No 1, (2018), p. 63–76, 2018, ISBN:
    9783838212296,

Pietrzak, Piotr. 2018. "Book Review: Immanuel Kant's
    Categorical Imperative and his Perpetual Peace: A
    Philosophical Sketch (1795)," *In Statu Nascendi –
    Journal of Political Philosophy and International
    Relations* Vol 1, No 1, (2018), ISBN:
    9783838212296,

Pietrzak, Piotr. 2018. Book Review: Charles P. Webel,
    (2004) Terror, Terrorism, and the Human
    Condition, New York: Palgrave Macmillan, *In
    Statu Nascendi – Journal of Political Philosophy
    and International Relations* Vol 1, No 1 (2018), p.
    207–214, 2018 ISBN: 9783838212296,

Pietrzak, Piotr. 2018. Edward Luttwak on the 2016
    Turkish Coup d'État Attempt: Insights and
    Recommendations, *In Statu Nascendi – Journal of
    Political Philosophy and International Relations*
    Vol 1, No 1 (2018), p. 215–224, ISBN:
    9783838212296,

Table of Contents